COMMON AMNESIAS

Praise for COMMON AMNESIAS

Common Amnesias is thrilling. A dizzying marathon through the taboo, the shamed, the disgusting. Cuff takes us far beyond shock value to deep intimacy. Rather than make a parade of shame, her poems seek to protect & value "the girl stored in tupperware / My call to keep her alive." Cuff writes, "Like the word river spelled backwards, I fall into myself." In her vertigo, shame's valuables are strapped to her chest: desire, depression, shitting, the very act of feeling. As she falls backwards, never landing, she grasps for a railing: "What to make of my inheritances—personal, familial, medical, cultural, racial?" As she repeatedly fails to secure a railing, we overhear her urgency, not just to survive this life, but to properly care for it. Her speaker, like a "woman [who] plants tulips in her yard with a pick ax," is simultaneously tender & voracious, troubled & troubling. *Common Amnesias* gripped me, challenged me, & provoked my stitching to come undone. I simply have never read anyone like Cuff.

—Shira Erlichman

Common Amnesias is quest through the underworld meets game night. This book points to behaviors that can't be called love or nature, the operations of the body, and what goes unsaid in families. Alex Cuff questions bravery. Thinking of "all the hamsters who have died without reason" and how "the land grab continues," she assembles things irrelevant enough to be poetry: "spuds," "cigarette money," "electrical tape," and a "bathrobe." And then she declares war.

—Joshua Escobar

These communities of text came to be and coalesced through the engine of quiet courage. They are brave and kind amid discomfort; they let shame go its petty distance and no further; they are nimble and patient in search of solutions. Alex Cuff's debut collection of poems fears no feeling and seeks freedom.

—Adjua Gargi Nzinga Greaves

Alex Cuff's *Common Amnesias* is a profound thinking-through of family—what it walls off, what it papers over, and the wondrous precarity of what's left: "My family did not discuss feelings / But my mother would often ask / About my movements / 'How are your bowels?' she'd say / In a tone of near accusation." There are brilliant, cumulative arguments tended in here, among them an appraisal of growing up in an environment (i.e., Long Island) where having an inner life is something to apologize for. Cuff's book is full of wonderfully sharp, quick-witted associations that comment hilariously on the uselessness of the shame they'd have you layer ("when i was nine i said hi in the mirror and was embarrassed"). Or maybe it's not about family at all, but the intelligence that persists beyond anything that would dull it, all those obstacles like "chairs from my hips and doors from my wrists / I walk through the house dislodging." Instant classic!

—Jacqueline Waters

Common Amnesias
© Alex Cuff, 2024

ISBN 978-1-946604-07-1
First Edition, First Printing, 2024

Ugly Duckling Presse
The Old American Can Factory
232 Third Street #E-303
Brooklyn, NY 11215
uglyducklingpresse.org

Distributed in the USA by Asterism
Distributed in the UK by Inpress Books

Typeset by wrongfoot
Cover illustration by Nina Yuen
Cover and inside cover designed and printed letterpress by IngeInge at Ugly Duckling Presse
Printed and bound at Sheridan (Saline, MI)

Common Amnesias

Alex Cuff

Ugly Duckling Presse
Brooklyn, NY

Family, A Natural Wonder	11
How Are Your Bowels?	33
Even Robocop Dreams of His Assassins	59
I Try Out a Sentence to See Whether I Believe	83

for my parents and siblings

FAMILY, A NATURAL WONDER

In America we have only the present tense. I am in danger. You are in danger.

—Adrienne Rich

DIRT

I am digging up potatoes and find the mother
Like all mother spuds it's rotten to the core
Like it, I have to be sacrificed
So that others can live
This guy says he likes when I'm sexy
He calls me Simone instead of Alex
In my mother's dining room
The blue-ribboned wallpaper
This guy pulls out his dick
Swings it toward my stomach
I know I'm in big trouble
If I pay the slightest attention
The wallpapered room is a small rocky cliff
A peninsula surrounded by water
Someone has set up a cocktail lounge
On the seafloor I dive down
I mix a drink
I am drunk with the lions
Their manes are humiliating
Ten years searching for that spot
Waiting in line for a public bathroom
I remember the girl stored in tupperware
My call to keep her alive
I'm hanging off a dead man's leg

His body attached to the crag of a mountain
A heavy wind bends us back like a lever
We snap and crash onto the rocks
The man's body crumbles like dry mud
I spy a living man hiking up the hill
Ask him to save me
My mother accuses me of trading
Danger for sex she is naked
And wrapped in saran wrap
I'm told that I will die by hanging
I stress about which pants to wear for the event
The exposure of my body
The twisting and turning of the rope
My mother hangs the windows with drapes
The room fills with smoke
My daughter asks me to change into a polka dot skirt
I visit the Jefferson branch of the library
I'm confused by her request
I study the past until I am learned and silent
When the house is demolished
I let others pick up the pieces
My daughter approaches
Okay okay I'm ready now
I stack two-by-fours
A man invites me to his private library
He shows me a white tome titled HERE AND NOW

He explains the premise
A collection of logical fallacies
I'm prohibited from reading
He says I owe him dinner for his brilliance
We like our women the way they are
I follow his logic and pick up the check
Butter both sides of a roll
Double up the body bag
I think of all the hamsters who have died
   without reason
When autumn ends I settle on winter's length
Nothing is slated to happen for years
Chairs from my hips and doors from my wrists
I walk through the house dislodging
I stand armed in the kitchen until morning

FAMILY, A NATURAL WONDER

we couldn't agree   on a location
                            to dispose the body
                            so we didn't

    we stuffed organs into Costco-sized jars of maraschino cherries

        we sensed humor   where there was some

we wept collections of TNT
we failed

                            before we thought

                            to act

                            our failures
                            came in

                                large
                                            and
                                                manageable
                            pieces

THE VILLAGE

Some wondered if pure love made it difficult to kill the neighbors.

A girl fixes peanut butter and jelly at a round oak table.
A girl fixes meatloaf on white toast with butter and pepper.
A girl fixes ham and swiss on rye.
A girl fixes turkey lettuce tomato and mayo on whole wheat.
A girl fixes roast beef on white.
A girl fixes salami and cheese on potato bread.
A girl fixes two eggs and American cheese on a kaiser.

That is a lie a girl says of the plain water tower
of the hand that holds her head underwater.
She sits at a kitchen table with a man
in black leather ankle boots and mixes up
the fear of drowning with the joy of living.
The kitchen is held by four walls and a girl.
A girl rubs mink oil on black leather ankle boots.
The boots are real. Somewhere outside
men with guns piss in an alley. A girl fixes
salami and cheese on potato bread. Somewhere
down the road a house burns to the ground.

A woman plants tulips in her yard with a pickaxe.
She builds seagulls out of Budweiser cans
to experience lightness. Something about

needing to move down in order to move up.
The woman has a chance encounter with a man
who professes to be a doctor but turns out
to be the leader of a dozen villagers
who believe the flood is coming.

A woman stands with her lover in a fire swamp,
where the only way out is down. Her lover jumps
into the lightning quicksand. The woman stalls
and her lover dies of asphyxiation. Later on
the woman sees her lover's sisters at a party
on the village outskirts. The sisters throw
her coat in vomit and knock her bike over.

The village tires of its people. They walk
the streets waving like overgrown underwater
weeds. In the park no one distinguishes pigeons
from joggers or dogs from children.
Empty benches line the lake. A girl fixes
two eggs and American cheese on a kaiser.
On the street, girls with hope in compound words
line up outside the alchemist's office
to resolve their misunderstanding
of the word *stranger*.

The girls are angry and bored and passive
and blamed for their passivity.

They drink their parents' liquor
babysit and bus tables for cigarette money
wear tight cotton bodysuits
get yeast infections
give hand jobs
spend their Sundays at church
their Saturday nights drinking
vodka in the triangle of trees
where Route 1 meets the highway.

Men mapping a demolition
of the abandoned building along the canal
press their faces against the fence
to see the girls on the dock.
The water in the bay is black.
A girl fixes roast beef on white.
A blimp sails overhead with a message.
A wild boar is often held by a small dog.

One by one the girls get into the water.
They give the bay their dissent.
One hundred years later
when the girls climb the shore
the men drop rolling
in the sand snorting
like small horses.

A WILD BOAR IS OFTEN HELD BY A SMALL DOG

Dining on vodka and roast beef, neapolitan ice cream and mashed potatoes
The family unit followed cues and ate its way through the world
A father in the back seat of the car exclaiming *I ate all the peanuts!*
His head filling the rearview mirror

NOUN NOUN

I have all these text messages from my father of phrases he thinks are funny because they are two nouns acting as adjective noun like store coffee store coffee is coffee that isn't brewed at home but at a store that you drink out of a cup with a lid and the milk and sugar are provided by the store some people call this to-go coffee he equates store coffee with loose coffee I disagree and say that loose coffee is ground before it is brewed not at all store coffee loose coffee is coffee made at home it is home coffee he says quidquid whatever I say box tea tea in a box of individually wrapped tea bags I say I am coming home to see you he says what time is your return train I search for the phrase *nouns that act as adjectives* on the internet and hope for a grammarian term something proper but the internet only says that sometimes we use a noun to describe another noun in which case the first noun acts as an adjective like ticket office race horse tennis ball I don't always know what to make of noun on noun and sometimes just want a descriptive word to accompany the noun like spotted egg or hollowed horse though I understand why some are wary of description thinking that description is not knowing not necessarily in any real sense of knowing the behind-the-scenes knowledge anyway and now and again when someone says *it is what it is* I lose faith that people will ever say what they mean he says I want to be a better father but I have no money he says don't tell your mother about the DUI you know because of her nerves he says at least I never hit you sleep socks boat shoes chicken egg grammarians might call this a compound noun the internet warns that a car accident is not an accident of the car he says people will ask why eve didn't

come to uncle ed's funeral I say tell them the truth she's not doing well
I say you two should finish the steps together he says we need to be
on the same page try this she didn't come to the funeral because she
is working I say but she doesn't have a job he says we have to return all
our vehicles to the neutral zone by 5:30 he says semper mihi hillae which
I translate as *I am a species all to myself* but he says no semper mihi
hillae means *hot sausages are always mine* I say that's a strange thing
to say to your daughter he says coffee snack dinner foil water boots

THE DIE HAS BEEN CAST

when I was nine I said *hi* in the mirror and was embarrassed
I hadn't known there were so many of us
I had dental anger, a tame handshake, and scotch tape
I'd been a champion of self-rule and early warning signs
togetherness, shitting, and vanity
curfews to prevent the disquiet
of her majesty's good subjects
when everyone left I'd hang back
to pet their soft sex
their wounded pink assholes
I'd rub their little ears
that guy at the train station
talking about his jolly green giant
what did you say? I said
he said *what would you say if I told you*
my jolly green giant
as if he hadn't told me
and I'm naturally mouthing words
naturally in costume
under a car channeling
I'll get in any body of water in front of the whole world
my therapist calls me a cheater
you're a cheater huh?
the hairdresser takes my hair in her hands like it's a limp dick
asks how long since I washed it

my body's changing color like the ponies of oz
and the line on the ground is a laser
is a crack
a scratch
a charcoal mass
is a ginger root
a green jaw
and nothing more
I'll get a coffee on a friday morning
I'll drive to west virginia with my mother
we'll listen to all 24 books of the odyssey
in pennsylvania she'll tell me to do
as calypso does to odysseus
keep a man in a cave, use medicinals

A COMMON AMNESIA

white butcher paper wrapping the white bagel with white sesame seeds inside white wax paper white spray paint tagging the framing store on main street six white people in the bagel store white napkins the white nissan sedan parked across the street left over dirty white snow before 1691 the word did not exist the white help wanted sign in the bagel store window me sitting under the bright white light bulb the pistachio ice cream green even though it is supposed to be white finding a way to be invisible when it needs to be before 1691 the word did not exist in a legal document the white november sky the white sign reading 8 miles no passing the white macbook charger soon to be obsolete plugged into the white power strip the white faux down comforter with ink stains and cat hair in 1691 the word was used for the first time in a legal document previously the christian and english indentured servants were referred to as christian and english indentured servants but then they were called white light on the white windowsill the white plastic coffee lid embossed with the letters S-O-L-D then the indentured servants who did not have black or brown skin came to be called white white drugs all the white noise white pages white backs of family pictures grey splinters of graves in the white blue snow whiteness was extended to landless europeans separating their condition from those of african descent encouraging them to hold their heads a little higher I'd say it was a pretty successful move even today I see some white folks holding their heads a little higher even if we won't remember why the large white book about the sun coconut oil white when solid the white part of the eye

THE TITLE OF THIS POEM IS THE VIRGINIA STATUTE OF 1691 STATES THAT WHOSOEVER ENGLISH OR OTHER WHITE MAN OR WOMAN, BOND OR FREE, SHALL INTERMARRY WITH A NEGRO, MULATTO, OR INDIAN MAN OR WOMAN, BOND OR FREE, HE SHALL WITHIN THREE MONTHS BE BANISHED FROM THIS DOMINION FOREVER.

        my mother says there's nothing
        wrong with marrying one
        except it would be selfish
        to not think of the children

FROM AN AERIAL VIEW THE FAMILY UNIT IS MADE UP OF INDIVIDUALS CORRESPONDING TO THEIR ENVIRONMENT

In a car, I once told my mom that if I opened a motel, I would call it the Sunrise Motel. I must have been thinking about the Brook Motel on Sunrise Highway and how the Patel family who went to St. Joseph's Elementary School and lived in and owned the Brook Motel didn't call it the Patel Motel, which would have rhymed. I often drink too much wine on Thanksgiving and end up in arguments about race at the dinner table. My mother changes the subject by telling me that I should not be allowed to teach sex ed to my 9th grade students because I'm not a certified health teacher. My mother's a nurse and before my 11th grade prom, while holding her hand to shield my eyes from a shower of aerosol hairspray, reminded me to keep my legs closed. In 2008 she gave me a navy blue floor-length robe for Christmas because a bathrobe is a respectable and practical garment to wear around the house after a shower, especially if you are a grown woman living with other adults, which I am. For my 37th birthday, she mailed me a card with a newspaper clipping about a woman who was caught with 37 cats in her Brooklyn apartment. The woman gave up the cats voluntarily and wasn't charged with any crime. My mother has since given me three blue robes. My favorite robe has a hood, is synthetic, and I smoke in it so much I'm surprised I haven't set myself on fire.

DESIRE

The road to becoming less disgusting is a long one but doable
Is what my Tinder profile says
I'm on the toilet swiping left and right
I schedule an event in my Google Calendar for October
Hello from March things aren't so great
I try to write a poem and am like *oh hi mom and dad*
All my poems are about a shame so deep I didn't shit for two weeks in college
The field is dead or built over or really far away or too expensive or there's not enough time
I give myself my first enema
I pour room temperature coffee into a lemonade pitcher and take it upstairs to the bathroom
I do a test run with a hot water bottle that doubles as a douche bag to ensure I can utilize the clamp correctly
I hang the bottle from its hook to a hanger on the shower and lie on my side with my iPhone
I rub coconut oil over my asshole
I raise a leg and slide the tube between my thighs
I stick the plastic nozzle into my ass
My cat Paolo watches skeptically after being shooed away from trying to smell my pussy
Contrary to what I'd read on the internet I didn't feel a surge of liquid fill my colon
Sadly I didn't feel anything really

But it worked

Big time

So I'm on the toilet flipping through the Skymall catalog

The Skymall catalog is selling the cooling pillow

Is selling the temperature regulating blanket

Is selling the genuine Turkish bathrobe

The original sleep sound generator

The nighttime arthritis pain-relieving gloves

The circulation-improving leg wraps

The turn your pool into an enchanting Venetian canal

Is selling the handmade steel promise cross signifies his love

The personalized center for exceptional grandchildren and children doormats

The finally your dog has a yard of its own

The she dreams of fairies now she can be one too

Is selling the your name in the sand

The track everything from your child to your most prized possession

The hands-free gear clock

The I can't promise sign

The say goodnight to bunions

Not for nothing but what if instead of saying *have a good one*

We just said, I can't promise you anything, or

Your name in the sand, man

LET'S GO SWIMMING

If you dress in disguise
and enter a distressing situation
you may be obliged to remain
based on a false premise

The man walking on water
rifle slung over shoulder
serves as a warning

Somewhere   someone   is using flattery
Somewhere   someone   is talking

                                  about killing a squirrel
                                        needing a haircut
                                                  pulling a curtain closed

If the water is coated in sulphuric outer space foam   I will get in

If the water is garrisoned with empty Dorito bags cigarette butts and
    rows of voyeurs

I will get in the water

The thought of coming up stands in conflict
with the distance between you and the surface

Eye contact like smoking is near impossible underwater

I'm thinking about making important decisions for us

If we act now
things can stay dry
for a long time

HOW ARE YOUR BOWELS?

    cultivating
     interior
   life
  sounds nice
 a rock needed to
float out of my body
 it seemed to know the way
  the password
  is Gravity
no need to whisper

—CAConrad

As a child I could not stand the anticipation of being found
I would jump out from hiding places during games of hide-and-seek
"I'm here!" I'd volunteer and desperately untangle myself from the
   dresses in my mother's closet

On Valentine's Day in 1997 I purchased anal beads for my college
    boyfriend J
He refused to participate
Saying something along the lines of "I will not put those in my butt"
I can't remember anything else from that night
Or the rest of that semester actually
I'm still not sure what my condition is
To counter the onset of a sinking mood
I consider making a list of ten things in which I have faith
I know for sure that pooping everyday won't be on the list

My family did not discuss feelings
But my mother would often ask
About my movements
"How are your bowels?" she'd say
In a tone of near accusation

Last month I sent my mother an image of an I POOPED TODAY t-shirt
She texted back "Gross!!!!!!!!!"
Then I texted her this tidbit since my condition is hereditary:

> *In truly serious cases constipation can be a symptom of an impacted bowel caused by a large dry lump of feces that's stuck in your colon*
> *In very rare cases straining to push it out can kill you*

One side effect of constipation is "emotional stagnation"
A tendency to produce incomplete ideas
Sentences insufficient in their ability to create meaning

I write sentences while standing
Because I have sprayed dissolved magnesium
All over my lower body

My sentences are often too heavy on the subject
The word *sentence* from the Latin infinitive sentire   to feel
How are you feeling? My thighs are burning

My cat Karl was spending excessive time in his litter box
Once I ruled out a UTI, I naturally suspected he was constipated
When the vet asked for evidence
That Karl might be constipated

    I tilted my chin forward
    then up
    stretched my arms out in front of my body
    at a 45 degree angle

She waited
But when I didn't say anything asked
"He's straining?"
I nodded

The fastest way to absorb magnesium into the body
Is through the skin
If you can handle the sting and itch
Handling the sting and itch is crucial
Especially if there is a chance that your large intestine
Has stopped absorbing nutrients

My partner calls from the bathroom to ask how to say *I am taking my second shit* in Italian

                        Sto facendo cacca per la seconda volta oggi!

The position of sitting spread over a hole
While it slides or is pushed out
The smell produced
The sound hitting the water
A blurred distinction between the act
Of shitting and an inexplicable shame
What began in the bowels soon spread
Until my skin itself electrified an unknowing
So frightening there were few ways back
One of them to disintegrate until skin lost
Its surface or whatever skin relies on to know anything

I dream about how hard it is to get off the ground as a bird

Once when I lay down loudly for too long
My therapist prescribed medication
      She said I was leaky
I was leaking but not through any orifice just psychically
I was awash in slippery fluids but my holes were paper dry

If depression is my slow landslide into darkness
Lightness is my large intestine dutifully performing
Its undulation of peristalsis as a joyful muscular tunnel

I entered my freshman year of college
As a biology major for no good reason as they say
The classes were rigorous but I was not
In the habit of studying so did not do well

I took a one-credit medical vocabulary course
All about Latin and Greek etymology and switched
Swiftly to the Classics department

The words and their origins beat the body and its systems

I have no memory of studying biology
Except that the small intestine has more
Beautiful name parts than the large intestine

jejunum and ileum

      vs

rectum and colic flexure

The light from my large intestine is one thousand years old

I have time

I eat a burrito at the Parade Grounds

Go to the dollar store

Find a glass bowl with a lid for school lunches

I spend the month abstaining

Abstain from alcohol in July

Abstain from alcohol for most of July

I purchase a blue translucent plastic spray bottle from Duane Reade

I make this purchase with great hope and promise

Spray my thighs in dissolved magnesium

I infuse herbs and drink tea

Tulsi & wood betony

Yellow dock & fennel

Burdock & prickly ash

I have time on my hands

I lose ground and wrestle

I mistake privilege for symptoms

I mistake the outside for the inside

Things ppl tell you when you are constipated:

    sit on the toilet at the same time each day

    it's common in women

    fiber up

    don't be embarrassed

In a dream I apply a band of black liquid eyeliner and wait
For my college boyfriend J to return to his dorm room
Meanwhile my sister Sarah uses his bathroom for a *long* time
Then leaves a minute before I hear his key card slap against the door

I meditate on the relationship between constipation and fear of a lover's fear of anal

The average bowel movement is three parts water to one part solid matter
When a woman breaks water she has a baby
When a man breaks water he gets rich
And so my relationship to water is clear
I advertise my water and provide notice of appropriation
I submit a proposal for an extension attesting that my water is really mine
Not some tributary some smaller part of another thing
Not a stadium-sized swimming pool that turns out to be the lap of a man driving the bus

While having loosened its total grip on my psyche, the constipation is still in charge

> If my large intestine has stopped absorbing nutrients
> due to a layer of shellac
> from years of not pooping
> then WHO AM I?

I'm in the bathtub with my brother Brendan

small brown turds   begin to float   to the surface   of the water

   someone shrieks   as if   there are

          sharks   emerging

In the eighties my dad called me a commie pinko for putting ketchup on
    my scrambled eggs
The magnesium is working
But there are still abstractions
I cannot absorb into the skin
I blow-dry the hair on my labia
Then my armpits
Then my bangs
For thirty seconds a piece in that order
Until everything on my body
Is more or less dry

EVEN ROBOCOP DREAMS OF HIS ASSASSINS

Hoofprint, lichen, slugs on rubble:
All that's left of the old rooms, crumpled.
—Doireann Ní Ghríofa

A CONSEQUENCE OF BELIEVING

Let me tell you about this dream I had

There was a horse show

People showing horses like

Look at me

I'm on a horse

I can make it

jump over things

There was hay

I held a bunch of it in my hands

THE SPACE IN BETWEEN

I dreamt a name disappearing like the tail of a large rodent
turning a corner I have nothing but a diminishing line
& a warning to not go through the motions
in my 20s I learned the phrase γνῶθι σεαυτόν is inscribed
on the Temple of Apollo at Delphi it translates
into English as *Know Thyself* what an impossible
invitation I thought now I think knowing the name
is less important than the experience of the space
in between the space in between having known a name
I no longer know & the disappearance of a rodent's tail

TRYING TO REVERSE THE SPELL

I have systems of interruption when my lack of belief is strongest

I stop to enter into routines most of which include my body

Like filling a stainless steel pot of water   lighting the stove
                    with a wooden match   pouring water
                          into a jar
                          of loose tea

                          sometimes the tea is black or
                          green sometimes it is a
                          combination of flowers roots
                          and seeds

Sometimes the routine calls for me on my back

          knees pulled up to my chest   then spread
          toward my shoulders   from this position

                                        I see only sky

I lipsync myself to sleep trying to reverse
the spell that wiped out my aggression

I dream I murder a girl and my mother covers up the crime
I cut out her pink tongue and chewy vocal cords

I throw her and her parts overboard into a sea
My mother finds the body and sews it up

I am embarrassed that I have dreamt something
as literal as my mother's complicity in my reticence

I practice integrating shame into my open throat
I wake in pine and chew tiny pieces of boiled ginger

Feel the spice work into my gums
A man explains to me the concept of *survival of the fittest* and its effects
    on the we

Stopping a man's chatter is like coaxing wet wood to spark into a
    devouring fire
I wake slick with sweat

A leaf on a tree trembles to hold on and I can stand myself when others
    are not around
Something happened to my jaw during the night and my teeth are
    smooth enamel

The summer I bought the blue plastic spray bottle from Duane Reade
I reread Mary Carruthers' *The Book of Memory* in an attempt to investigate
The relationship between memory lapse and spiritual despair

In medieval Europe memory was a mark of moral character as well as
    intellectual superiority
In Ancient Greek the word we translate into English as to read is *anaginosko*
To know again or *to recollect*

In Latin the word we translate into English as *to read* is *legere*
To collect, choose, or gather as if all the knowing already exists
And can simply be assembled through an act of reading

I break from an act of reading and allow my body to experience its grief

To not remember what I've read is what I imagine it is like
To plummet through space and not die

The possibility of knowing flies past bright and beautiful as fire

I dream the Guggenheim Museum drifts down the East River on a barge
Followed by the 6th Avenue Jefferson branch of the library

The subject of my anxiety shifts and lands on what is most socially palpable
I take the advice of several friends who say it is ok to not get out of bed

The contradiction of my own brain   *take it easy girl   get the fuck off the floor*

When the priest in my hometown church mentioned Pope Gregory was also known as Gregory the Great, my mom leaned over and whispered *Gregory the Great was a Hildebrand. Grandpa always said we were of papal lineage.*

My mom's "maiden" name is Hildebrand. According to Wikipedia, Gregory Hildebrand is not *the* Gregory the Great but was a pope nonetheless; in fact, he was the first pope "to rigorously enforce the Western Church's ancient policy of celibacy for the clergy."

The Gregory the Great on the other hand was a medieval "intellect" known for converting pagans to Christianity.

He instructed:

>*There are some so restless that*
>*when they are free from labor*
>*they labor all the more because*
>*the more leisure they have for thought*
>*the worse interior turmoil they have to bear.*

The question of whether I will kill another geranium does not keep me
   from sleeping
The question of how belief may be fastened to keeping things alive does
   not keep me from dreaming

Some days I am more fragment than story more abstraction than image
An impatient host to a restlessness that language cannot pin down

Periods of acute anxiety make it nearly impossible   to locate an
                                                                                 internal coherence
                                                                                 in the company
                                                                                 of other humans

Journal entry from May 10th: Don't cower

Journal entry from May 15th: Take the list and feast

HUMAN ANIMAL MACHINE

I abandoned human
moved outside my body brushed
my eyelashes better to see
you see me
and we got along fine
both of us having that amnesia
that lets us bring things into the body
take them out
and move them around the house

I watched movement witnessed transaction
at 3:03 a shadow cut the building in half
at 3:10 the sun went in
the building stood whole again
or so I thought
when I see a thing
I make it real

a woman naturally smoking in the hallway
a woman naturally standing at a table counting money
a woman naturally tyrannizing a room of windows
a woman naturally at the bottom of a river
a woman naturally in a sunroom confessing to all the plants

a small white room
on the ground floor
pillows stacked like cats
here and there color
a dog barking
the bed and a dust ruffle
the dresser and its weight
the clapboard dusty
the bed a pair of wire-framed glasses
a light bed
built for one
as if we're expected to die
in our sleep wearing shoes
in the bed masturbating
the room is a giant aperture
the mattress is very expensive

a large dog and the small of my neck
a water-soluble paradox
the rooms are connected
the damage is muzzled
dreams are not accidental
a pencil cactus
slanting rectangles of paper
they come built into the rooms
I walk across the room toward the door

I knock into a piece of furniture
I don't want to be sentimental
but I walk across the room
and objects move out of my way

the dog had me by the neck
the man was shirtless
the kitchen floor was cracked
the man was blond and bearded
the dog was toothed
the door opened from the inside
the motion was not a magician but a man
not (a) disappearance but (b) invisibility
the writing on the wall was in Greek
the nails on the wall held nothing visible
a crash of motorcycles projected miniature
the kitchen floor was cracked
the man had me by the neck
the miniature was not so miniature up close
the magician was shirtless
the dog cracked
the crash opened from the inside
the motion was not a magician but a floor

POSSESSION

I exit the B train at Herald Square and step onto the escalator
I feel my heartbeat where I imagine my lungs should be and most likely are

So much for dispossession as a political act
I'm talking about a lack of self-possession as an involuntary act

My large intestine has stopped absorbing nutrients so I'm sweating into a magnesium bath
I meditate on the intersection between the collective amnesia of settler colonialism

And my own failure to retain what I learn
I self perform a labia massage

My memory is poor thanks in part to explosions of cortisol at the mother's disappearing act
I consider the relationship between absorption and waste removal

This land accumulates in my heart, and in my pension through the teacher's union
I've stolen everything I'll ever call mine

Claudia Rankine wrote "white can't know what white feels"
My whiteness says *mine*

I study how to love my family outside the myth in which it's been sown
I give up on loving to understand and settle for loving to heal

A girl on the escalator with purple flowers and a suitcase
A girl on the bus in a yellow dress, flowers on the dress, and me
   counting all the flowers

Me in a lake and from the lake the only flowers are the umbrellas on shore
And my small brain flower and the warm piss between my legs floral

EVEN ROBOCOP DREAMS OF HIS ASSASSINS

I bite into an egg and cheese and my temporary crown and its odor
Roll through my mouth like a coin loosed in a washing machine

Mrs. K said dreams of fallen teeth are a sign of a death to come
Which deaths am I not already mourning

When I was young there was a house and then it was gone
I dream a young boy pinched my ass and it came off in his hand

The dentist taps my shoulder three times and refuses me pain meds
I discover my mouth is just another hole

Sweetheart, have a glass of wine, take a tylenol
My anger shimmers—now it's here, now it's shame, now it's somewhere else

I renounce my go-to substances and return to preteen mourning
I get a root canal while Christine Blasey Ford testifies before Congress

My mouth frothy under a rubber dental dam
I dream my dad into a low-key heroin addict

An addiction as soft and temperate as a salt bath
Any harm caused is just magnesium dissolved into the big picture

ORDINARY FEATS

Like the day we arrive at a pool
Scraps of fabric ride the slide, clog the filter, line the bottom of the pool
We talk about swimming and you feed me a piece of soft cheese
We find the suburbs unchanged and nobody is held accountable
The wind is stiff so we build a garage in which we place our linen and family members
A girl measures the length of a room and asks us to remove our shoes
It is difficult to say no to that which is still living
Racing to answer the phone does not bring us closer to the person who is calling
Our change in scenery may be misread as resignation
Sounds of a lawnmower are different sounds from those of a bird
There are some bird nests that raise suspicion of artifice
In this way we learn about desire
We understand that flashlights are tools and rooms have seams where a ceiling meets a wall
That sharing features with siblings explains nothing about storms along the equator
Not sleeping has become a form of labor
Some landscapes benefit from intervention
This may or may not imply infidelity
We undress and remove our shoes
We peel paisley from the slide and make a wet feather bed at the bottom of the pool

In some dreams a person may act the way they act in real life
This is an ordinary feat on the part of the dreamer

SUSPICION OF ARTIFICE

As a child I rejected the belief in things I could not see
I believed in the bats living in the basement but did not believe in communism
My beliefs had the weight of the material world: sun-warmed backyard dirt, my grandmother's glass of whiskey and her milky eye, a heavy regenerative breath into the mouth of a Nintendo cartridge
In those days I needed time to fortify belief
These days I need time to dismantle it
My family spent the nineties climbing over furniture
My siblings and I tried to stay out of the way because my parents believed in the Eternal Law, which promises wretched lives to evil men
We assumed this law applied to evil children as well
We lived in the moment but not like Zen masters
We canceled the future out with the past
Or at least that's how I see it now, looking back, a line-drive sort of existence, a difficulty, not in adhering to beliefs, but in remembering what they are
We held our breath and prayed for the best, making exterior a shared fear of loving
And living happened under anaerobic conditions
This might've fucked me up if I hadn't had a few of my own beliefs, mainly in things that I could see, like difference between a man-made lake and a bathtub
I learned difference early on and when I could see it, I made it real

The color of a maraschino cherry was not the color of a real cherry
    and the order in which siblings were born—first middle second fifth
    second to last—I knew that too
I knew that warm-blooded vertebrates provided with wings are sometimes
    birds, but I couldn't conceive of flying bodies as non-bat objects
I thought of anything that flew outside my window as a nocturnal
    mammal with webbed wings
At the time my father lived in a den filled with green wicker furniture
The den fell under jurisdiction of Temporal Law which protects the things
    a man can lose
A sagging green chair legislated my father
He turned his will over to the bats living in the basement
The basement fell under jurisdiction of the Night, and of the Bats
In the Old Norse sense of the word husband, my mother was my father's
    husband
She held distress at bay with lilacs
She tried to protect us from the power of the den but her silence
    couldn't will it away
The room raged with free will and acid reflux
In '88 my parents put the chain lock on the basement door before I'd
    reached the top of the stairs
My change in scenery read as resignation
I coveted the potential violence of baking soda and vinegar
I doubted windows
I mixed drinks
I mounted chairs

I made pinpricks
I snapped doors
I bent flukes
I said yes to what was still alive
I did not murder someone with a colander of pinto beans
I did not recline into a spread eagle on the cold floor
I stood still and let a few pieces of grass fall between my fingers
In '98 the house burned to the ground
No one died but everyone was hurt

I TRY OUT A SENTENCE TO SEE WHETHER I BELIEVE

Where
In this architecture of dust
Will you find the space to build
A house that does not split?

—Jackie Wang

It's early in the year, early in the week, early in the day.
A man clips his fingernails on the L train.
I think about outrage at the public act of hygiene.
I think *I've done worse.*
Done more damage than that with my thoughts.
I begin at the graveyard where the sun is low in the sky.
I put my things into the flatness where I can see them.

Here we are orange tractor someone's digging up a grave.
Like the word river spelled backwards, I fall into myself.
My histories have me in fits.
Another death by drowning dream.
Another death by asphyxiation dream.
Another death by public sex dream.

I dream my parents at a gas station. I fail to leave before they see me.
I'm wearing a very wet bathing suit.
Somehow it's clear to everyone that I've been having sex.
With lots of people.
Young men with long eyelashes cross the street into the sun.
I think *we're not all in this together.*

Yesterday I was too stunned too sad too in a way feeling the sadness.
Today I am too stunned too sad too in a way not feeling the sadness.
I participate in the whitest lockdown of collective wonder.
Seeing my fingers in the metal, I fear my fate is sealed.
I'm all those assholes.
Having things I don't want to be told to not have.
A thin rope in my back pocket, I am ready to strangle the truth out of anyone.

I dream a large man trying to get to my pussy. My wonder and slight disgust at his ball sack.

The theory that every person in one's dream is actually the dreamer.

Sentimental men continue to scare me.

I do not want to help them.

However I am a trooper for custom.

When a man says without prompting *just because I'm a guy, doesn't mean I'm an idiot* I don't respond.

Suddenly I have systems.

Erotic green scallops growing out of a tree trunk.

I become horny when I enter a greenhouse.

When I came upon marsh fern, I knew water was near.

Or that if water were not near, I need to worry.

Sometimes Earth is so obscured I forget her.

My heart goes out to the new year sidewalk tree massacre.

I try out a sentence to see whether I believe: I can't find my nature.

My lover puts the entirety of my foot into his mouth and fries leeks.
I'm waking up to paternal etymologies. I'm solving problems on the ice.
I want to eat the buttery carrots, the shag carpet, and the long road to
   the graveyard.
There's some good on the individual level but not enough courage.
Dear courage, I'm crushed by fear of scarcity.
I keep a to-do list on my phone. Go to the pine trees. Find water. Try harder.
I spend 17 dollars on two sweet potatoes, a dozen eggs, cremini
   mushrooms, and a can of beer.
I know some to think me a heathen.
I have no plan but having nothing in the fridge feels wrong. I'm bored
   with my performances.
The cat-dog argument, the superiority of the drugless body, the one up,
   the who's your daddy, the tightrope.

I read a story about a man who struggles to support his consumptive wife
    and her long ropes of hair by digging graves and collecting scrap metal.
I thought it was a bad story but find myself wondering where I can get a
    wife with long ropes of hair.
Consumptive or not everyone I know is dying.
I cross *dye things green* from my to-do list.
I am in the produce aisle at Key Food.
I am hushed by a man who has his hands deep in the bananas.
I make synaptic space for future threats.
I see sap in the trees so I tap them.

I am still unclear about pancakes and the appropriate amount to eat in one sitting.
I am still unclear about the difference between my symptoms and my privileges.
When I am tired I sit on public toilet bowls.
I am privately putting things in my holes.

I see the machine bodies as antiquated for the first time.
I strangle someone to death in a dream.
The Wilson graveyard leaning in.
The Wilson graveyard smooth silvery silicone.
I want my body to be the first to go.
No.
I want a partially visible body.
If a man comes inside who shouldn't come inside, redeem your things.
And if a man comes inside who shouldn't.
And if a person has you so that you can only speak in syllogisms.

I dream about a father with a broken back.

Surprise. He's alive.

When the idiosyncratic language family plan goes bankrupt.

When you want to purchase several services and you do.

When you can't tell the difference between a maraschino cherry and whatever gets off in formaldehyde.

My therapist says I'm brave to keep trying to be close to humans.
The work of social being double duty.
I'm holding in my moisture, waiting for it to drop.
The forecast: industrial plastic whipping a gentrified storm.
And not one of us but both of us we all disappear.

I have a poor memory. This alone tests belief.

I read books and cannot retell or synthesize what I've read.

Ideas I take in through the reading process might as well be dreams from my past lives.

When I am tired I experience what my mother calls the heebie jeebies—restlessness in my leg muscles, as if my body is complaining about its lack of options.

There is no such thing as not having a past but I've lived a long time in this way.//
I am not saying that this is a poem.
One could say that my father has lived ahistorically.
Did so when he protested the protesters of the Vietnam war.
Says *a bunch of spoiled rich kids what did they know.*
I teach my students the letter "a" can be a prefix and we look at the words *atypical atonal asymptomatic.*
I have lived for a long time unaware of my symptoms.
Like in 1492 Columbus sailed the ocean blue.

In the eighties I attend St. Joseph's elementary school.

I am a terrible student. The adults are dismayed.

I work hard to memorize the definitions of treaty, egalitarianism, and democracy.

I did not get the D in D-Day, could not memorize the causes and effects of World War I.

Who signed the Treaty of Versailles? Who was the Archduke Ferdinand and what did he have for breakfast on the morning of his assassination?

I keep reminding myself to put my arms down. That there's enough for
    everyone.
On the L train seated facing south, my view is field, path, grave, and tree.
Khalilah Brann said, "History accompanies my body into the room."
I try out that sentence to see whether I believe.
On the L train west toward Union Square.
Three boys dance, they throw handsprings, they tell us to not worry.
That no one will get hurt.
That everyone is safe.

A wide road runs through the graveyard midway between the Wilson Avenue and Bushwick-Aberdeen stations.

The road goes until you can no longer see it by which time it has another name.

I reach into my bag and discover sharp items I'd written off as stolen.

I lament that a beer glass is not the same as a glass of beer and go to the corner for a six pack.

I try out a sentence: There are few reasons beyond intergenerational wealth that people are rich.

I live in the city where people show signs of their richness.

Like not eating food if the food doesn't taste good. A one-way ticket to faraway places.

Like taking an apartment or not taking an apartment. Working or not working.

Privilege is rigid but its language is like air.

Imagine having everything you need for you and your pets. Access to professionals. Flaunted symmetries.

I'm soothed by the intake process of any appointment.
I want to sit across from someone in a professional relationship and believe they are the expert of my life.
I will answer all their questions about age, medical history, sleep patterns, employment, and diet.
Something about the limits of bureaucracy grant me permission to resign any effort to change anything outside whatever I have to do to arrive in that chair.
I try out a sentence to see whether I believe: Not every hand on deck is necessary.
I want things and my destination subsumes the encounter.
I dream gymnastics camp. The head coach thinks my name is Jennifer Mackenzie.
I take comfort thinking that Jennifer Mackenzie sounds like a person with a lot of rights, and flexibility.

When I meet beautiful people with means I think about meritocracy, citizenry, and survival of the fittest.

I am attracted to monotony.

I still cannot truly say whether knowing the thing that afflicts can lessen the hold of the affliction.

I could be asking the wrong questions.

I try out a sentence to see whether I believe: The labor of others is the fullness of my weekend.

I'm a dangerous receptacle with all this ego.

I may not be strong enough to wrestle my symptoms.

I try out a sentence: You may not be strong enough to wrestle your symptoms.

It doesn't matter that conspiracy is to breathe together.
That insolence is to be brave.
That darkness is to hold.
We may be so satisfied we never want to change a thing.

At a young age I learned to never ask anyone about his financial business.

I took that off the table of casual conversation.

I'm often in fear that bodies near me will transform into the Incredible Hulk, that green muscular irrationality.

The land grab continues.

LA is burning just like Octavia Butler said it would. Genocide in the Dakotas, still.

I finish Delany's *Dhalgren* and experience a listlessness.

I have doubts that I will know how to transition back into the real world.

A world in which excessive violence has not brought down capitalism.

A world in which catastrophe has not granted me more sex.

I am learning the outlines of hunger and how they chameleon.

In 1988 I saw Devin Murphy's balls hanging out of his shorts while he drove a motor boat through the Long Island Sound.

In 2000 I woke up alone in Adam Siegel's bed with menstrual blood everywhere. I laid down electrical tape to create an outline of my gone body.

In 2010 a man whose name I've lost visited me in Brooklyn.

I put him in my bed and slept on the couch.

The next morning he left the city and a Trojan Magnum on my pillow.

I guess he wanted me to know what I was missing.

There are several ways to imagine a body.

I continue to perform in the face of my histories.

A provisional history. A history arranged or existing for the present, possibly to be changed later.

A provisional belief. A belief arranged or existing for the present, possibly to be changed later.

A provisional sentence. A sentence arranged or existing for the present, possibly to be changed later.

On some days when I try out a sentence to see whether I believe, no one dies.

I dream my mother wants to pee into my teal Jansport backpack.
I turn 40 and dream of swimming. The water dreams return in full.
Water I am not allowed to jump into.
Water obstacle courses that end in a bubbling lap lane all for me.

I dream of taking two stairs at a time.
I want to push my nails into something soft and have someone stop what they are saying.
My own smallness my constant compass.
One bright yellow tree at the Wilson Avenue station.
I scan my body or whatever it is I rely on to know anything.
And I am jettisoned into caring.

NOTES

A Common Amnesia and *The Title of This Poem Is The Virginia Statute of 1691* were inspired by the book *In the Matter of Color: Race & the American Legal Process: The Colonial Period* by A. Leon Higginbotham Jr., introduced to me by Dr. Michael Washington, a facilitator with the People's Institute for Survival and Beyond (PISAB).

The line in *The Village* and the poem title, *A Wild Boar Is Often Held By a Small Dog*, and the poem title *The Die Is Cast*, are translations from Latin aphorisms found in *Latin for Reading: A Beginner's Textbook with Exercises*: "A cane non magno saepe tenetur aper" attributed to Ovid and "Alea jacta est" attributed to Suetonius.

How Are Your Bowels? was birthed as a somatic ritual in the spirit and brilliance of CAConrad, via invitation from Sara Jane Stoner in the *ALL INSEPARABLE NOW* workshop at Wendy's Subway in 2017.

The poem *A Consequence of Believing* is titled after the line, "Knowing is a consequence of believing" in the poem, "At dinner you wore a beautiful sweatshirt" by Aisha Sasha John.

In *Trying to Reverse the Spell*, the Mary Carruthers book mentioned is *The Book of Memory: A Study of Memory in Medieval Culture*, introduced to me by Lisa Jarnot in her Pattern Poetry workshop in 2009.

Human Animal Machine borrows the lines "a small white room / on the ground floor" from the opening narration of Chantal Akerman's 1974 film *Je Tu Il Elle*. Much of the poem was made from dreams I had after viewing the film.

The line "white can't know what white feels" is from Claudia Rankine's poem *Sound & Fury*, which I had written down on a napkin after hearing her read at BAM on May 9, 2017.

The seeds of *I Try Out a Sentence to See Whether I Believe* were a one-line-a-day text exchange with Adjua Gargi Nzinga Greaves in 2015.

The line "I see sap in the trees so I tap them" is borrowed from the first lyric of the song *Sycamore* by Bill Callahan: "There's sap in the trees if you tap 'em."

Shaherah Khalilah Brann (1979–2018) was an activist, educator, scholar, mentor, and founder of *CREAD: Culturally Responsive Educators of the African Diaspora*. She left us too soon, but her light shines.

ACKNOWLEDGMENTS

Love and gratitude to so many—all of whom are my teachers—who have encouraged, cared for and held space for these poems, including: Genji Amino, Mirene Arsanios, Daisy Atterbury, Alana Baum, Marie-Helene Bertino, Pranav Behari, Anselm Berrigan, Emily Brandt, Sean Breidenthal, Mahogany L. Browne, Jamie Chan, Chia-Lun Chang, Jacob Ciocci, Charity Coleman, Ian Dreiblatt, R. Erica Doyle, Cornelius Eady, Mel Elberg, Shira Erlichman, Joshua Escobar, Camonghne Felix, Rob Fitterman, Adam Fitzgerald, t'ai freedom ford, Rico Frederick, Jordan E. Franklin, Alexis Garcia, Yasamin Ghiasi, Renee Gladman, Adjua Gargi Nzinga Greaves, Anna Gurton-Wachter, Michelle Gurule, Haoyan of America, Siri Helleloid, Zakia Henderson-Brown, Laura Henriksen, Rachel Higgins & Charlie, Tiffany Houck, Lucy Ives, Greyson Hong, Lisa Jarnot, Sana Khan, Steven Karl, Nina Keller, Marie La Viña, Anne Lai, Ann Lauterbach, Zoe Leonard, Layli Long Soldier, Dan Magers, Cynthia Manick, Jessica Millnitz, Anna Moschovakis, José Olivarez, Leila Ortiz, Eric Pitra, Noel Quiñones, Matana Roberts, Marianne Shaneen, Sara Jane Stoner, Roberto Tejada, Jacqueline Waters, Nicole Shanté White, Stephanie White, Lauren Whitehead, Morgan Võ, Matvei Yankelevich, Ariel Yelen, and Nina Yuen.

Thanks to the editors of the following publications, where versions of these poems were published: *Apogee Journal*, "A Common Amnesia"; *The Brooklyn Rail*, "I Try Out A Sentence to See Whether I Believe"; *Diner Journal*, "The Village"; *The Fanzine*, "Desire"; *Leveler*, "Let's Go Swimming"; *Los Angeles Review of Books*, "Suspicion of Artifice," "Poetry & the Body"; *Poet's House*, "The Title Of This Poem Is The Virginia Statute Of 1691"; *Poetry Project Newsletter #243*, "Human Animal Machine"; *The Recluse*, "Dirt," "Noun Noun," "From an Aerial View the Family Unit Is Made Up of Individuals Corresponding to Their Environments," and "The Die is Cast." And to REALITY BEACH and Ghost Proposal for publishing chapbooks that house many of these poems.

Endless appreciation to everyone at UDP, especially Lee Norton and Kyra Simone for their spacious editorial guidance, and Milo Wippermann for their magical design powers.

Thank you to Nina Yuen for hundreds of intestinal drawings.

Oceans of gratitude to mom, dad, Lauren, Sarah, Brendan, and Liam for humor, language, and love. And to Dave Sargent, Karl, Kuma, Paolo, and all the plants, for making tender room for all of us.